Catholic Mass Notes
for Kids

My Mass Notes

_____

_____

_____

Today's Date: _____

Church Date: _____

What color are the Priest's
vestments today?

_____

Liturgy of the Word

Where is the 1st reading from today? Old or New Testament

Book Chapter: Verse _____

Responsorial Psalm:

_____

Where is the 2nd reading from today? Old or New Testament

Book Chapter: Verse _____

Gospel Acclamation:

_____

Where is the Gospel reading from today?

Book Chapter: Verse _____

What was the homily about:

_____
_____
_____
_____
_____
_____

How can I apply this in my life?

_____
_____
_____
_____

Draw about todays lesson
or one of the readings:

Did anything special happen today?

Date: _____

Homily Notes:

_____
_____
_____
_____
_____
_____
_____
_____
_____
_____
_____
_____
_____

Something we prayed for today:

Two songs we sang were:

Draw about todays lesson:

What other names for God and Jesus did you hear today?:

☐ Lord   ☐ Son of God

☐ Father   ☐ Savior

☐ Almighty   ☐ Shepherd

☐ Creator   ☐ Lamb of God

Where were the readings from today?

Today's Date:

_____

Church Date:

_____

What color are the Priest's vestments today?

Today's readings and homily:

What are we learning about Jesus:

_____
_____
_____
_____
_____
_____

How does this help me or teach me?

_____
_____
_____

Today I prayed for:

One of todays readings was from:

Book: _____

Chapter/Verse: _____

Draw about a reading today:

What did you hear today that you don't understand?

_____
_____
_____
_____
_____

What was your favorite song today? Why?

_____
_____
_____
_____
_____
_____
_____

Date:

Who gave the homily today?

_____

Today's homily:

What are we learning about God:

_____
_____
_____
_____
_____
_____

How can I use this in my life?

_____
_____
_____

Today I prayed for:

One of todays readings was from:

Book: _____

Chapter/Verse: _____

Draw about a reading today:

What did you hear today that
you don't understand?

_____
_____
_____
_____
_____
_____

What was your favorite song today? Why?

Today's Date: _____

Church Date: _____

What color are the Priest's vestments today?

_____

Liturgy of the Word

Where is the 1st reading from today? Old or New Testament

Book Chapter: Verse _____

Responsorial Psalm:

_____

Where is the 2nd reading from today? Old or New Testament

Book Chapter: Verse _____

Gospel Acclamation:

_____

Where is the Gospel reading from today?

Book Chapter: Verse _____

What was the homily about:

_____
_____
_____
_____
_____
_____

How can I apply this in my life?

_____
_____
_____

Draw about todays lesson
or one of the readings:

Did anything special happen today?

Date: _____

Homily Notes:

_____
_____
_____
_____
_____
_____
_____
_____
_____
_____
_____
_____

Something we prayed for today:

Two songs we sang were:

Draw about todays lesson:

What other names for God and
Jesus did you hear today?:

☐ Lord   ☐ Son of God

☐ Father   ☐ Savior

☐ Almighty   ☐ Shepherd

☐ Creator   ☐ Lamb of God

Where were the readings from today?

Today's Date:

_____

Church Date:

_____

What color are the Priest's vestments today?

Today's readings and homily:

What are we learning about Jesus:

_____
_____
_____
_____
_____
_____

How does this help me or teach me?

_____
_____
_____

Today I prayed for:

One of todays readings was from:

Book: _____

Chapter/Verse: _____

Draw about a reading today:

What did you hear today that
you don't understand?

_____
_____
_____
_____
_____

What was your favorite song today? Why?

_____
_____
_____
_____
_____
_____
_____

Date:

Who gave the homily today?

_____

Today's homily:

What are we learning about God:

_____
_____
_____
_____
_____
_____

How can I use this in my life?

_____
_____
_____

Today I prayed for:

One of todays readings was from:

Book: _____

Chapter/Verse: _____

Draw about a reading today:

What did you hear today that you don't understand?

_____
_____
_____
_____
_____
_____

What was your favorite song today? Why?

Today's Date: _____

Church Date: _____

What color are the Priest's vestments today?

_____

Liturgy of the Word

Where is the 1st reading from today? Old or New Testament

Book Chapter: Verse _____

Responsorial Psalm:

_____

Where is the 2nd reading from today? Old or New Testament

Book Chapter: Verse _____

Gospel Acclamation:

_____

Where is the Gospel reading from today?

Book Chapter: Verse _____

What was the homily about:

_____
_____
_____
_____
_____
_____

How can I apply this in my life?

_____
_____
_____

Draw about todays lesson
or one of the readings:

Did anything special happen today?

Date: _____

Homily Notes:

_____
_____
_____
_____
_____
_____
_____
_____
_____
_____
_____
_____

Something we prayed for today:

Two songs we sang were:

Draw about todays lesson:

What other names for God and Jesus did you hear today?:

☐ Lord   ☐ Son of God

☐ Father   ☐ Savior

☐ Almighty   ☐ Shepherd

☐ Creator   ☐ Lamb of God

Where were the readings from today?

Today's Date:

_____

Church Date:

_____

What color are the Priest's vestments today?

Today's readings and homily:

What are we learning about Jesus:

_____
_____
_____
_____
_____
_____

How does this help me or teach me?

_____
_____
_____

Today I prayed for:

One of todays readings was from:

Book: _____

Chapter/Verse: _____

Draw about a reading today:

What did you hear today that
you don't understand?
_____
_____
_____
_____
_____
_____

What was your favorite song today? Why?
_____
_____
_____
_____
_____
_____
_____

Date:

Who gave the homily today?

_____

Today's homily:

What are we learning about God:

_____
_____
_____
_____
_____
_____

How can I use this in my life?

_____
_____
_____

Today I prayed for:

One of todays readings was from:

Book: _____

Chapter/Verse: _____

Draw about a reading today:

What did you hear today that
you don't understand?

_____
_____
_____
_____
_____

What was your favorite song today? Why?

Today's Date: _____

Church Date: _____

What color are the Priest's vestments today?

_____

Liturgy of the Word

Where is the 1st reading from today? Old or New Testament

Book Chapter: Verse _____

Responsorial Psalm:

_____

Where is the 2nd reading from today? Old or New Testament

Book Chapter: Verse _____

Gospel Acclamation:

_____

Where is the Gospel reading from today?

Book Chapter: Verse _____

What was the homily about:

_____
_____
_____
_____
_____
_____

How can I apply this in my life?

_____
_____
_____

Draw about todays lesson
or one of the readings:

Did anything special happen today?

Date: _____

Homily Notes:

_____
_____
_____
_____
_____
_____
_____
_____
_____
_____
_____
_____
_____

Something we prayed for today:

Two songs we sang were:

Draw about todays lesson:

What other names for God and
Jesus did you hear today?:

☐ Lord   ☐ Son of God

☐ Father   ☐ Savior

☐ Almighty   ☐ Shepherd

☐ Creator   ☐ Lamb of God

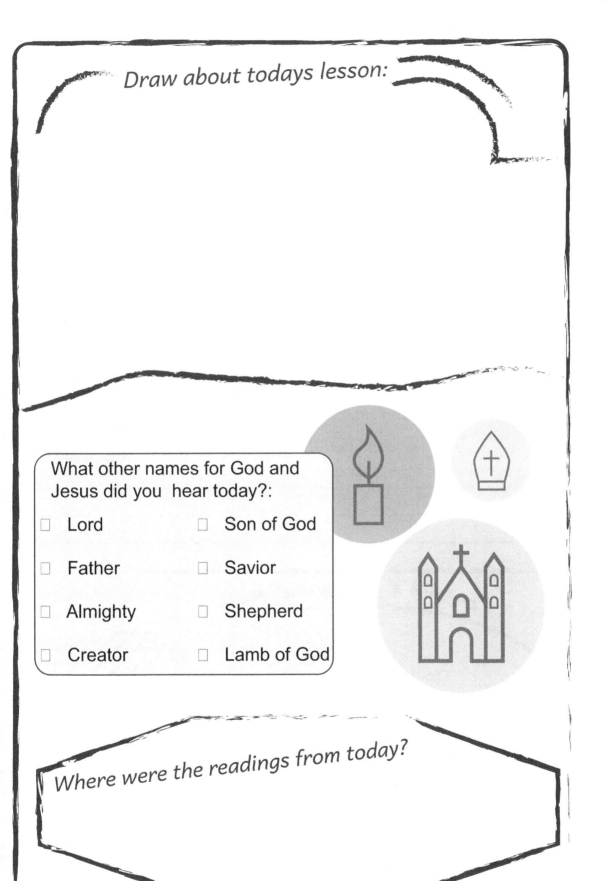

Where were the readings from today?

Today's Date:

_____

Church Date:

_____

What color are the Priest's vestments today?

Today's readings and homily:

What are we learning about Jesus:

_____
_____
_____
_____
_____
_____

How does this help me or teach me?

_____
_____
_____

Today I prayed for:

One of todays readings was from:

Book: _____

Chapter/Verse: _____

Draw about a reading today:

What did you hear today that you don't understand?

_____
_____
_____
_____
_____
_____

What was your favorite song today? Why?

_____
_____
_____
_____
_____
_____
_____

Date:

_____

Who gave the homily today?

Today's homily:

What are we learning about God:

_____
_____
_____
_____
_____
_____

How can I use this in my life?

_____
_____
_____

Today I prayed for:

One of todays readings was from:

Book: _____

Chapter/Verse: _____

Draw about a reading today:

What did you hear today that
you don't understand?

_____

_____

_____

_____

_____

_____

What was your favorite song today? Why?

Today's Date: _____

Church Date: _____

What color are the Priest's
vestments today?

_____

Liturgy of the Word

Where is the 1st reading from today? Old or New Testament

Book Chapter: Verse _____

Responsorial Psalm:

_____

Where is the 2nd reading from today? Old or New Testament

Book Chapter: Verse _____

Gospel Acclamation:

_____

Where is the Gospel reading from today?

Book Chapter: Verse _____

What was the homily about:

_____

_____

_____

_____

_____

_____

How can I apply this in my life?

_____

_____

_____

_____

Draw about todays lesson
or one of the readings:

Did anything special happen today?

Date: _____

Homily Notes:

_____
_____
_____
_____
_____
_____
_____
_____
_____
_____
_____

Something we prayed for today:

Two songs we sang were:

Draw about todays lesson:

What other names for God and Jesus did you hear today?:

☐ Lord   ☐ Son of God

☐ Father   ☐ Savior

☐ Almighty   ☐ Shepherd

☐ Creator   ☐ Lamb of God

Where were the readings from today?

Today's Date:

_____

Church Date:

_____

What color are the Priest's vestments today?

Today's readings and homily:

What are we learning about Jesus:

_____
_____
_____
_____
_____
_____

How does this help me or teach me?

_____
_____
_____

Today I prayed for:

One of todays readings was from:

Book: _____

Chapter/Verse: _____

Draw about a reading today:

What did you hear today that
you don't understand?
_____
_____
_____
_____
_____
_____

What was your favorite song today? Why?
_____
_____
_____
_____
_____
_____
_____

Date: _____

Who gave the homily today?

Today's homily:

What are we learning about God:

_____
_____
_____
_____
_____
_____

How can I use this in my life?

_____
_____
_____

Today I prayed for:

One of todays readings was from:

Book: _____

Chapter/Verse: _____

Draw about a reading today:

What did you hear today that
you don't understand?

_____
_____
_____
_____
_____

What was your favorite song today? Why?

Today's Date: _____

Church Date: _____

What color are the Priest's
vestments today?

_____

Liturgy of the Word

Where is the 1st reading from today? Old or New Testament

Book Chapter: Verse _____

Responsorial Psalm:

_____

Where is the 2nd reading from today? Old or New Testament

Book Chapter: Verse _____

Gospel Acclamation:

_____

Where is the Gospel reading from today?

Book Chapter: Verse _____

What was the homily about:

_____
_____
_____
_____
_____
_____

How can I apply this in my life?

_____
_____
_____

Draw about todays lesson
or one of the readings:

Did anything special happen today?

Date: _____

Homily Notes:

_____
_____
_____
_____
_____
_____
_____
_____
_____
_____
_____
_____

Something we prayed for today:

Two songs we sang were:

Draw about todays lesson:

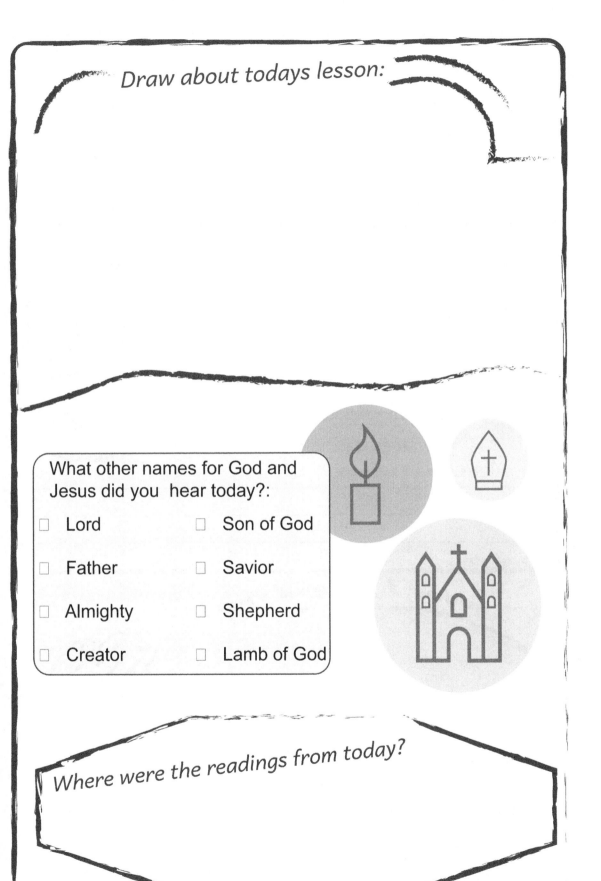

What other names for God and Jesus did you hear today?:

☐ Lord   ☐ Son of God

☐ Father   ☐ Savior

☐ Almighty ☐ Shepherd

☐ Creator   ☐ Lamb of God

Where were the readings from today?

Today's Date:

_____

Church Date:

_____

What color are the Priest's vestments today?

Today's readings and homily:

What are we learning about Jesus:

_____
_____
_____
_____
_____
_____

How does this help me or teach me?

_____
_____
_____

Today I prayed for:

One of todays readings was from:

Book: _____

Chapter/Verse: _____

Draw about a reading today:

What did you hear today that you don't understand?
_____
_____
_____
_____
_____
_____

What was your favorite song today? Why?
_____
_____
_____
_____
_____
_____
_____

Date:

_____

Who gave the homily today?

Today's homily:

What are we learning about God:

_____
_____
_____
_____
_____
_____

How can I use this in my life?

_____
_____
_____

Today I prayed for:

One of todays readings was from:

Book: _____

Chapter/Verse: _____

Draw about a reading today:

What did you hear today that you don't understand?

_____
_____
_____
_____
_____
_____

What was your favorite song today? Why?

Today's Date: _____

Church Date: _____

What color are the Priest's
vestments today?

_____

Liturgy of the Word

Where is the 1st reading from today? Old or New Testament

Book Chapter: Verse _____

Responsorial Psalm:

_____

Where is the 2nd reading from today? Old or New Testament

Book Chapter: Verse _____

Gospel Acclamation:

_____

Where is the Gospel reading from today?

Book Chapter: Verse _____

What was the homily about:

_____
_____
_____
_____
_____
_____

How can I apply this in my life?

_____
_____
_____
_____

Draw about todays lesson
or one of the readings:

Did anything special happen today?

Date: _____

Homily Notes:

_____
_____
_____
_____
_____
_____
_____
_____
_____
_____
_____
_____

Something we prayed for today:

Two songs we sang were:

Draw about todays lesson:

What other names for God and
Jesus did you hear today?:

☐ Lord   ☐ Son of God

☐ Father   ☐ Savior

☐ Almighty   ☐ Shepherd

☐ Creator   ☐ Lamb of God

Where were the readings from today?

Today's Date:

_____

Church Date:

_____

What color are the Priest's vestments today?

Today's readings and homily:

What are we learning about Jesus:

_____
_____
_____
_____
_____
_____

How does this help me or teach me?

_____
_____
_____

Today I prayed for:

One of todays readings was from:

Book: _____

Chapter/Verse: _____

Draw about a reading today:

What did you hear today that
you don't understand?

_____

_____

_____

_____

_____

_____

What was your favorite song today? Why?

_____

_____

_____

_____

_____

_____

_____

Date:

Who gave the homily today?

_____

Today's homily:

What are we learning about God:

_____
_____
_____
_____
_____
_____

How can I use this in my life?

_____
_____
_____

Today I prayed for:

One of todays readings was from:

Book: _____

Chapter/Verse: _____

Draw about a reading today:

What did you hear today that you don't understand?

_____
_____
_____
_____
_____
_____

What was your favorite song today? Why?

Today's Date: _____

Church Date: _____

What color are the Priest's
vestments today?

_____

Liturgy of the Word

Where is the 1st reading from today? Old or New Testament

Book Chapter: Verse _____

Responsorial Psalm:

_____

Where is the 2nd reading from today? Old or New Testament

Book Chapter: Verse _____

Gospel Acclamation:

_____

Where is the Gospel reading from today?

Book Chapter: Verse _____

What was the homily about:

_____
_____
_____
_____
_____
_____

How can I apply this in my life?

_____
_____
_____
_____

Draw about todays lesson
or one of the readings:

Did anything special happen today?

Date: _____

Homily Notes:

_____
_____
_____
_____
_____
_____
_____
_____
_____
_____
_____
_____

Something we prayed for today:

Two songs we sang were:

Draw about todays lesson:

What other names for God and Jesus did you hear today?:

☐ Lord   ☐ Son of God

☐ Father   ☐ Savior

☐ Almighty   ☐ Shepherd

☐ Creator   ☐ Lamb of God

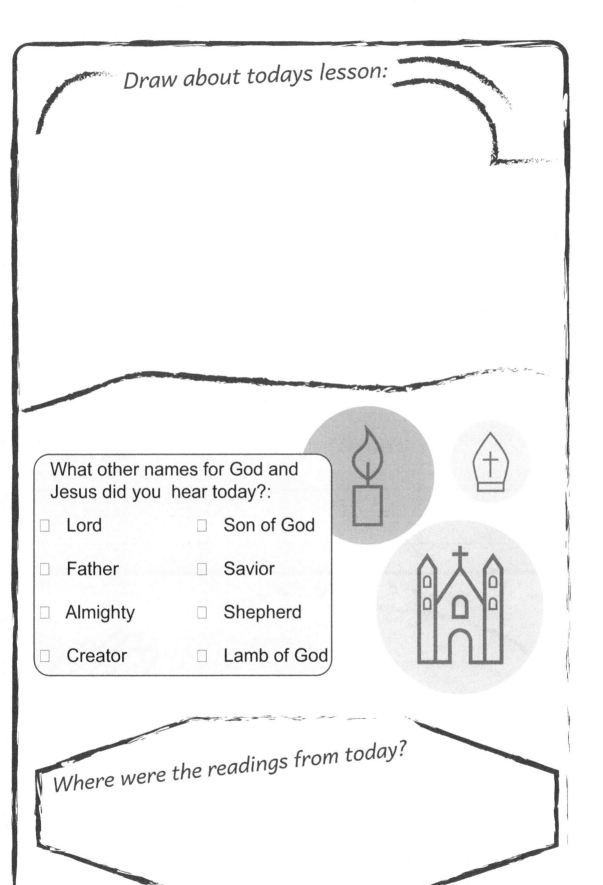

Where were the readings from today?

Today's Date:

_____

Church Date:

_____

What color are the Priest's vestments today?

Today's readings and homily:

What are we learning about Jesus:

_____
_____
_____
_____
_____
_____

How does this help me or teach me?

_____
_____
_____

Today I prayed for:

One of todays readings was from:

Book: _____

Chapter/Verse: _____

Draw about a reading today:

What did you hear today that
you don't understand?
_____
_____
_____
_____
_____
_____

What was your favorite song today? Why?
_____
_____
_____
_____
_____
_____

Date:

Who gave the homily today?

Today's homily:

What are we learning about God:

_____
_____
_____
_____
_____
_____

How can I use this in my life?

_____
_____
_____

Today I prayed for:

One of todays readings was from:

Book: _____

Chapter/Verse: _____

Draw about a reading today:

What did you hear today that you don't understand?

_____

_____

_____

_____

_____

What was your favorite song today? Why?

Today's Date: _____

Church Date: _____

What color are the Priest's vestments today?

_____

Liturgy of the Word

Where is the 1st reading from today? Old or New Testament

Book Chapter: Verse _____

Responsorial Psalm:

_____

Where is the 2nd reading from today? Old or New Testament

Book Chapter: Verse _____

Gospel Acclamation:

_____

Where is the Gospel reading from today?

Book Chapter: Verse _____

What was the homily about:

_____
_____
_____
_____
_____
_____

How can I apply this in my life?

_____
_____
_____

Draw about todays lesson
or one of the readings:

Did anything special happen today?

Date: _____

Homily Notes:

_____
_____
_____
_____
_____
_____
_____
_____
_____
_____
_____
_____
_____
_____

Something we prayed for today:

Two songs we sang were:

Draw about todays lesson:

What other names for God and Jesus did you hear today?:

☐ Lord   ☐ Son of God

☐ Father   ☐ Savior

☐ Almighty   ☐ Shepherd

☐ Creator   ☐ Lamb of God

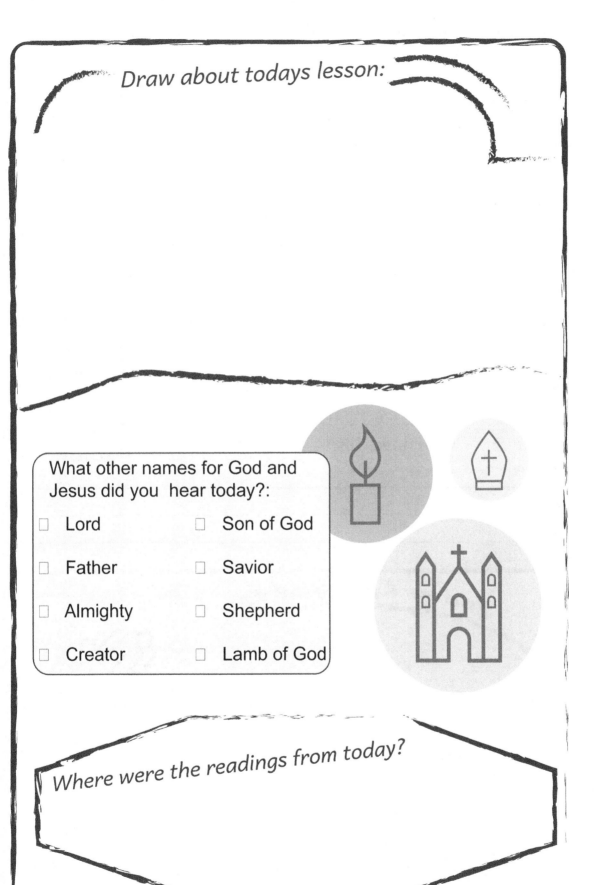

Where were the readings from today?

Today's Date:

_____

Church Date:

_____

What color are the Priest's vestments today?

Today's readings and homily:

What are we learning about Jesus:

_____
_____
_____
_____
_____
_____

How does this help me or teach me?

_____
_____
_____

Today I prayed for:

One of todays readings was from:

Book: _____

Chapter/Verse: _____

Draw about a reading today:

What did you hear today that you don't understand?

_____

_____

_____

_____

_____

_____

What was your favorite song today? Why?

_____

_____

_____

_____

_____

_____

_____

Date:

Who gave the homily today?

Today's homily:

What are we learning about God:

_____
_____
_____
_____
_____
_____

How can I use this in my life?

_____
_____
_____

Today I prayed for:

One of todays readings was from:

Book: _____

Chapter/Verse: _____

Draw about a reading today:

What did you hear today that
you don't understand?
_____
_____
_____
_____
_____
_____

What was your favorite song today? Why?

Today's Date: _____

Church Date: _____

What color are the Priest's
vestments today?

_____

Liturgy of the Word

Where is the 1st reading from today? Old or New Testament

Book Chapter: Verse _____

Responsorial Psalm:

_____

Where is the 2nd reading from today? Old or New Testament

Book Chapter: Verse _____

Gospel Acclamation:

_____

Where is the Gospel reading from today?

Book Chapter: Verse _____

What was the homily about:

_____

_____

_____

_____

_____

_____

How can I apply this in my life?

_____

_____

_____

Draw about todays lesson
or one of the readings:

Did anything special happen today?

Date: _____

Homily Notes:

_____
_____
_____
_____
_____
_____
_____
_____
_____
_____
_____
_____
_____
_____
_____

Something we prayed for today:

Two songs we sang were:

Draw about todays lesson:

What other names for God and
Jesus did you hear today?:

☐ Lord   ☐ Son of God

☐ Father   ☐ Savior

☐ Almighty   ☐ Shepherd

☐ Creator   ☐ Lamb of God

Where were the readings from today?

Today's Date:

_____

Church Date:

_____

What color are the Priest's vestments today?

Today's readings and homily:

What are we learning about Jesus:

_____
_____
_____
_____
_____
_____

How does this help me or teach me?

_____
_____
_____

Today I prayed for:

One of todays readings was from:

Book: _____

Chapter/Verse: _____

Draw about a reading today:

What did you hear today that you don't understand?

_____
_____
_____
_____
_____
_____

What was your favorite song today? Why?

_____
_____
_____
_____
_____
_____
_____

Date:

Who gave the homily today?

_____

Today's homily:

What are we learning about God:

_____
_____
_____
_____
_____
_____

How can I use this in my life?

_____
_____
_____

Today I prayed for:

One of todays readings was from:

Book: _____

Chapter/Verse: _____

Draw about a reading today:

What did you hear today that
you don't understand?

_____
_____
_____
_____
_____
_____

What was your favorite song today? Why?

Today's Date: _____

Church Date: _____

What color are the Priest's vestments today?

_____

Liturgy of the Word

Where is the 1st reading from today? Old or New Testament

Book Chapter: Verse _____

Responsorial Psalm:

_____

Where is the 2nd reading from today? Old or New Testament

Book Chapter: Verse _____

Gospel Acclamation:

_____

Where is the Gospel reading from today?

Book Chapter: Verse _____

What was the homily about:

_____

_____

_____

_____

_____

_____

How can I apply this in my life?

_____

_____

_____

_____

Draw about todays lesson
or one of the readings:

Did anything special happen today?

Date: _____

Homily Notes:

_____
_____
_____
_____
_____
_____
_____
_____
_____
_____
_____
_____
_____

Something we prayed for today:

Two songs we sang were:

Draw about todays lesson:

What other names for God and
Jesus did you hear today?:

☐ Lord   ☐ Son of God

☐ Father   ☐ Savior

☐ Almighty   ☐ Shepherd

☐ Creator   ☐ Lamb of God

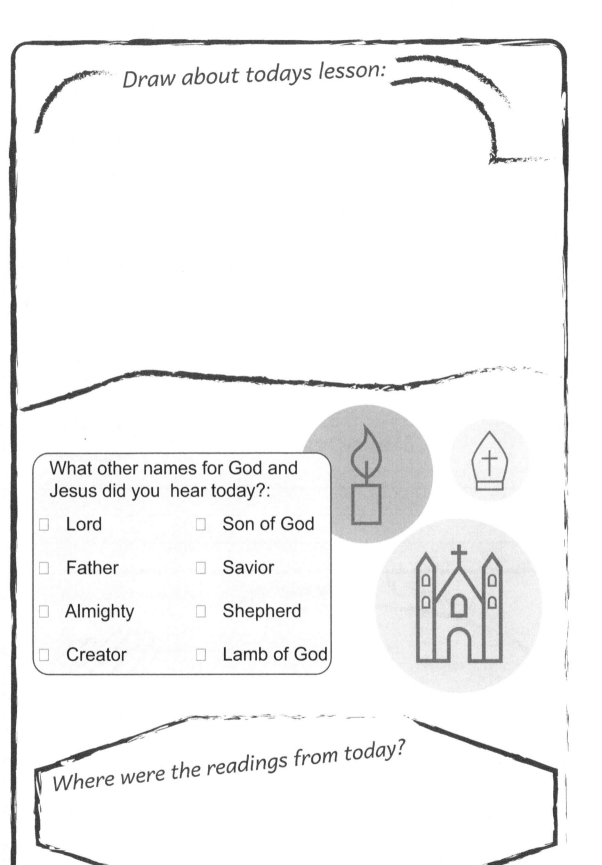

Where were the readings from today?

Today's Date:

_____

Church Date:

_____

What color are the Priest's vestments today?

Today's readings and homily:

What are we learning about Jesus:

_____
_____
_____
_____
_____
_____

How does this help me or teach me?

_____
_____
_____

Today I prayed for:

One of todays readings was from:

Book: _____

Chapter/Verse: _____

Draw about a reading today:

What did you hear today that you don't understand?

_____
_____
_____
_____
_____
_____

What was your favorite song today? Why?

_____
_____
_____
_____
_____
_____
_____

Date:

Who gave the homily today?

_____

Today's homily:

What are we learning about God:

_____
_____
_____
_____
_____
_____

How can I use this in my life?

_____
_____
_____

Today I prayed for:

One of todays readings was from:

Book: _____

Chapter/Verse: _____

Draw about a reading today:

What did you hear today that
you don't understand?

_____
_____
_____
_____
_____
_____

What was your favorite song today? Why?

Today's Date: _____

Church Date: _____

What color are the Priest's vestments today?

_____

Liturgy of the Word

Where is the 1st reading from today? Old or New Testament

Book Chapter: Verse _____

Responsorial Psalm:

_____

Where is the 2nd reading from today? Old or New Testament

Book Chapter: Verse _____

Gospel Acclamation:

_____

Where is the Gospel reading from today?

Book Chapter: Verse _____

What was the homily about:

_____
_____
_____
_____
_____
_____
_____

How can I apply this in my life?

_____
_____
_____
_____

Draw about todays lesson
or one of the readings:

Did anything special happen today?

Date: _____

Homily Notes:

_____
_____
_____
_____
_____
_____
_____
_____
_____
_____
_____
_____
_____
_____

Something we prayed for today:

Two songs we sang were:

Draw about todays lesson:

What other names for God and
Jesus did you hear today?:

☐ Lord   ☐ Son of God

☐ Father   ☐ Savior

☐ Almighty   ☐ Shepherd

☐ Creator   ☐ Lamb of God

Where were the readings from today?

Today's Date:

_____

Church Date:

_____

What color are the Priest's vestments today?

Today's readings and homily:

What are we learning about Jesus:

_____
_____
_____
_____
_____
_____

How does this help me or teach me?

_____
_____
_____

Today I prayed for:

One of todays readings was from:

Book: _____

Chapter/Verse: _____

Draw about a reading today:

What did you hear today that you don't understand?

_____
_____
_____
_____
_____
_____

What was your favorite song today? Why?

_____
_____
_____
_____
_____
_____
_____

Date:

Who gave the homily today?

Today's homily:

What are we learning about God:

_____
_____
_____
_____
_____
_____

How can I use this in my life?

_____
_____
_____

Today I prayed for:

One of todays readings was from:

Book: _____

Chapter/Verse: _____

Draw about a reading today:

What did you hear today that you don't understand?

_____

_____

_____

_____

_____

_____

What was your favorite song today? Why?

Today's Date: _____

Church Date: _____

What color are the Priest's
vestments today?

_____

Liturgy of the Word

Where is the 1st reading from today? Old or New Testament

Book Chapter: Verse _____

Responsorial Psalm:

_____

Where is the 2nd reading from today? Old or New Testament

Book Chapter: Verse _____

Gospel Acclamation:

_____

Where is the Gospel reading from today?

Book Chapter: Verse _____

What was the homily about:

_____

_____

_____

_____

_____

_____

How can I apply this in my life?

_____

_____

_____

Draw about todays lesson
or one of the readings:

Did anything special happen today?

Date: _____

Homily Notes:

_____
_____
_____
_____
_____
_____
_____
_____
_____
_____
_____
_____

Something we prayed for today:

Two songs we sang were:

Draw about todays lesson:

What other names for God and Jesus did you hear today?:

☐ Lord   ☐ Son of God

☐ Father   ☐ Savior

☐ Almighty   ☐ Shepherd

☐ Creator   ☐ Lamb of God

Where were the readings from today?

Today's Date:

_____

Church Date:

_____

What color are the Priest's vestments today?

Today's readings and homily:

What are we learning about Jesus:

_____
_____
_____
_____
_____
_____

How does this help me or teach me?

_____
_____
_____

Today I prayed for:

One of todays readings was from:

Book: _____

Chapter/Verse: _____

Draw about a reading today:

What did you hear today that
you don't understand?

_____
_____
_____
_____
_____
_____

What was your favorite song today? Why?

_____
_____
_____
_____
_____
_____
_____

Date:

Who gave the homily today?

Today's homily:

What are we learning about God:

_____
_____
_____
_____
_____
_____

How can I use this in my life?

_____
_____
_____

Today I prayed for:

One of todays readings was from:

Book: _____

Chapter/Verse: _____

Draw about a reading today:

What did you hear today that you don't understand?

_____
_____
_____
_____
_____
_____

What was your favorite song today? Why?

Made in the USA
Monee, IL
23 March 2021